Nehemiah

BUILDER FOR GOD

The Story of Nehemiah
accurately retold from the Bible
(from the Book of Nehemiah), by
NEIL M. ROSS

Design and Illustrations
Duncan McLaren
Mackay Design Associates Ltd

Published in Great Britain by
CHRISTIAN FOCUS PUBLICATIONS LTD
Geanies House, Fearn, Tain, Ross-shire IV20 1TW, Scotland
© 1983 Christian Focus Publications Ltd ISBN 0 906731 11 9

Published in Australia and New Zealand by
DAYSTAR *and distributed by* W. A. BUCHANAN & CO
21 Kyabra Street, Fortitude Valley, Brisbane, Q, Australia 4006
© 1983 Daystar ISBN 0 949462 02 0

Published in Nigeria by
AMAZING GRACE LTD
P.O. Box 173, Kano, Nigeria
© 1983 Amazing Grace Ltd

Co-edition arranged with the help of Angus Hudson, London

Long ago, in the land of Persia,
there was a rich and noble Jew
called Nehemiah who loved and
worshipped God.

He was the important servant,
called The Cup-bearer, of King
Artaxerxes of Persia and served
the king's wine to him.

King Artaxerxes ruled over many lands. One of these lands was Judah where the Jews lived and where the famous city of Jerusalem was.

One day, some Jews from Judah visited Nehemiah and gave him sad news.

They told him that the Jews there were being cruelly treated by their enemies and that the wall and city gates of Jerusalem were in ruins.

Nehemiah wept after hearing this.
What could he do? He did the best
thing he could have done, for he
prayed to God about it. He asked
God to help him to do something
for the Jews.

One day after this, Nehemiah was very sad as he served wine to King Artaxerxes.

"Why do you look sad?" the king suddenly asked him.

Nehemiah told the king the bad news about the ruined wall and gates of Jerusalem.

"What do you want?" asked the king.

Right away, Nehemiah prayed silently to God for help and then asked the king, "Please send me to Jerusalem to build its wall".

What do you think happened? The king not only granted him his wish but even made him Governor of Judah. How wonderfully God answered Nehemiah's prayers.

Do you have difficulties and troubles? Take them to the Lord in prayer because He can answer your prayers too.

When Nehemiah came to Jerusalem, two men were very displeased that he had come to help the Jews. Their names were Sanballat and Tobiah and they hated the Jews.

One night, soon after he came to Jerusalem, Nehemiah and some of his men secretly went to see how much work would have to be done to mend the city wall. How badly broken down it was! Heaps of stones and other rubble lay all around.

Nehemiah went to the chief men of the city and said, "Come and let us build up the wall of Jerusalem!" When they heard from Nehemiah how God had been helping him they were glad and wanted to start building.

So Nehemiah and the people began to build the wall. What a difficult job they had to do! The heaps of rubble had to be cleared away. The wall had to be built very high and wide right round the city. The Sheep Gate, the East Gate and the other eight gates of the city all had to be repaired.

Sanballat was in a rage at the Jews when he saw them start to build and he said that the wall would be useless. Tobiah also mocked them and said, "Even a fox, if it went up on the wall, would break it down".

But Nehemiah trusted in God and prayed to Him again for help. God answered Nehemiah's prayer and helped them to work so well that soon half of the huge wall was finished.

Sanballat and his wicked friends now became very angry. They made a plan to suddenly attack the Jews and stop them building.

Nehemiah heard about their wicked plan and prayed to God about that too. Then he made a plan to defend the city.

He ordered half the men to take their weapons and guard the city. The others were to keep on working but with their swords beside them. They were all to defend the city as soon as the trumpet would sound at the command of Nehemiah.

Because Nehemiah was trusting in God to help them in battle he told the people, "Our God shall fight for us". So the work went on and at the same time the city was guarded day and night. The men did not take off their clothes even at night, except to wash, so that they were always ready to fight.

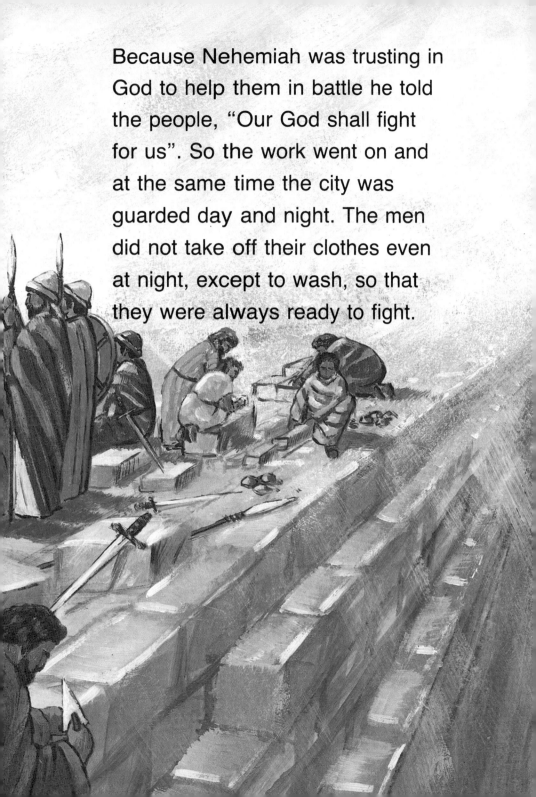

Nehemiah had another worry at this time. Some rich Jews lent money to many of the Jews who were poor. But they also took the land, houses and even the children from these poor Jews until the money was paid back. This was very wrong because God commanded them not to treat their brother Jews in this way.

The poor Jews told Nehemiah about it and asked him to help them. Nehemiah told the rich Jews, "It is not good that you do!" and pleaded with them to have pity on the poor Jews.

When the poor Jews heard that the rich Jews promised to give back their property and children they were very glad and praised God.

We also must pity the poor. God says to everyone that those who pity the poor lend to Him and that He will pay them back.

The wall was now nearly finished and Sanballat and Tobiah suddenly became very friendly to Nehemiah. They actually invited him to come down to visit them. Were they really friendly? Not at all, for they were secretly plotting to hurt him.

Nehemiah refused their invitation and sent a message to them saying, "I am doing a great work, so that I cannot come down".

Sanballat tried other evil tricks to frighten Nehemiah and stop the work, but each time Nehemiah asked God for help. So the people were helped to work on and on until the wall was finished.

Do you know how long they took to build that great wall? Only 52 days, because God made them willing and strong to build the wall of His city.

Some time after that, all the
people, children as well, met
together in one of the streets of
the city to worship God. Ezra the
priest and some of the other
priests stood on a big wooden
pulpit in front of the people and
read and explained God's law to
them.

We too must meet together to hear God's word, the Bible, explained to us by God's messengers, the preachers of the gospel.

When the people understood the meaning of God's word they worshipped God in the way that He wanted. They kept the holy feasts and they were really sorry for their sins.

We must be truly sorry for our sins and ask God to forgive us for Jesus' sake.

After that, the people promised
God that they would keep his
laws. This promise was written
down and Nehemiah and other
chief men wrote their names under it.

There was another big gathering
of the people: this time to thank
God for helping them to build the wall.

What a happy day that was!
Thousands of men, women and
children, led by Nehemiah and the
princes and the priests, praised
God with such great joy that they
were heard by those who lived far
away from the city.

We too should be thanking God for His goodness and especially for His greatest gift. What is that gift? It is the gift of His dear Son, Jesus Christ, whom He gave to save sinners.

After that happy day Nehemiah carried on governing Judah for some years and then went back to Persia.

But Nehemiah did come back to visit Jerusalem some time later. During that visit he saw some things which made him sad.

He saw that one of the rooms in
God's holy temple had been given
to wicked Tobiah to live in.
Nehemiah was very upset. He
threw Tobiah's belongings out of
the temple and did not allow him
to live there any longer.

Nehemiah also saw many of the people doing work on the Sabbath day that God had forbidden them to do on that holy day. He told the people how wrong they were. He also ordered the merchants, who came to the city to sell their goods on the Sabbath day, to go away. They did not come back again on God's day to sell.

We too must not do what God
forbids us to do on His holy day,
the Lord's Day, which is the
Sabbath day of Christians. God
still commands us, "Remember
the sabbath day, to keep it holy".

There was another thing which
made Nehemiah sad. Many Jews
had married heathen people.

God had forbidden them to do this
because the heathen did not
worship Him but worshipped idols.

Nehemiah punished those Jews
and made the people promise that
they would not allow their sons or
daughters to marry heathen
people.

Once more, Nehemiah put right some things that were wrong, praying to God for help to do so.

We see then that Nehemiah was a man who worked very hard for God and for God's people.

He was also a very brave man for he kept doing what was right even when some people hated him for that.

We must follow his example and do what God tells us to do, even when others try to stop us.

Above all, Nehemiah was a man of prayer. Again and again he asked God for His help and blessing and God answered his prayers.

Nehemiah wrote a book called *The Book of Nehemiah*, which you will find in the Bible. There you can read the story of Nehemiah and his work.

The last words of *The Book of Nehemiah* are a prayer that Nehemiah prayed.

You too can pray that prayer, for God promises you, "Ask and you shall receive".

Here is the prayer, "Remember me, O my God, for good".